"Wendy Maragh Taylor with her husband, traveled to Liberia, West Africa with the plan of building a church and school. This story is both a cultural journey into an area rarely seen by western eyes and an affirmation that despite our differences, we have much in common. And by climbing out of her comfort zone, Wendy, with her charming descriptions of her misadventures, learns a lot about herself. With an ending like no other, Wendy makes a call to action that is hard to ignore. May we all be inspired by This Part Of The Sky.*"*

— MJ Hanley-Goff, writer, editor,
Hudson Valley Parent | *Hudson Valley Life*;
and author of the upcoming *How Writing Can Get You Through Hard Times and Joyous Ones*

"We are honored. It is too fine. The whole town will read this book."

— Dennis Tarbo, Elder in Zorzor, Liberia

This Part Of The Sky

Building in Liberia

This Part
Of The Sky

Building in Liberia

Wendy Maragh Taylor

This Part of the Sky: Building in Liberia

Book Cover: Nick Zelinger, NZ Graphics
Editing: Donna Mazzitelli, Writing with Donna
Layout/Design: Andrea Costantine
Author Photograph: Joseph Taylor

Printed in the United States of America

First Edition
ISBN 978-1-479-22485-2

The people, events, and descriptions contained in this book are based on my journal entries and personal memories. The people's names, including their spelling, have been recorded to the best of my recollection and understanding. Loma is an oral language. All words and names in Loma have been spelled phonetically, based on how I heard them. Any incorrect or misspelled names are purely unintentional.

This book is dedicated to the people of Zorzor, Liberia. May your beauty continue to inspire us all.

Ga Galah mama a vai mah.

Table of Contents

The Power of Community

Over the past couple of years, my husband and I have been invited to share about the work we did with the Liberia Project. In our presentations, we talk about the process of fundraising, the work we did in Zorzor, and we show pictures from our time there. I also read excerpts from my journals. Consistently, people have offered positive feedback and encouraged me to publish our experience.

What a roller-coaster ride this book project has been—thrilling and nerve-racking at the same time. The initial draw to publish was my desire to share what took place, including the remarkable people I met in Liberia. I also saw this book as a great way to continue funding the additional work we plan to do—a percentage of the proceeds from its sale will go to the Liberia Project. Over time, I also envisioned *This Part Of The Sky* as a means to encourage others to do the work they talk about and long for—work that often seems too far from their reach. What I wasn't willing to do was alter my description of the events or people to make the book more marketable or a better-seller—as had been suggested to me. As well, I couldn't afford to pay an agent to "shop" my book to traditional publishers. Finally, the thought of giving up "the rights" to my own writing didn't appeal to me either.

After some research, Kickstarter—the world's largest funding platform for creative projects—seemed to be in perfect alignment with my decision to publish a book about the Liberia Project based on my journals. Working through Kickstarter was attractive to me for a couple of reasons. The challenge to get people involved by pledging financially in return for rewards related to the book or the Liberia trip felt exciting. And it seemed it could be fun as well—except for the part where I would receive none of the funding if this project didn't meet our financial goal within a certain time period. Thankfully, we did meet it—even surpassing the goal amount before the deadline date. The book project's "backers" are individuals and groups of family members, friends, and co-workers who have pooled their funds. The pledges ranged from $5 to $600.

I continue to be in awe of the ways individuals can come together to do extraordinary things. It's how Joseph and I funded the Liberia Project. Then, too, I was stunned that we raised $10, 000—donations ranged from $5 to $1,000. In both cases, we weren't able to go to businesses for large donations nor could we offer people tax deductions since we are not an organization. People gave simply because they wanted to help.

I'm extremely grateful for the involvement and support of family, friends, and colleagues, along with a few strangers—a community—all willing to give to others. What an amazing mark we can make on another community and in individuals' lives when we come together, as so many of us did on behalf of the Liberia Project. And...what a powerful impact it can have on us too!

"Whatsoever thy hand findeth to do,
do it with thy might."
– Ecclesiastes 9:10

Acknowledgments

This book was made possible because of the following Kickstarter backers listed below.

Thank you:

Emerson & Angela Piercy

Simone Coombs

Ursus A. Idosu

Inez & Ruth Niles

Joseph Bon Sesay

Gerald Charleston
Janice Edwards-Clarke
Gloria M. Gibbs
Alice Sesay Jalloh
Cathleen Kinn
Kirk & Donna Maragh
Terry & Ilene Osbourne
Clinton & Dianna Powell
Eldridge & Lisa Powell
Viola Stevens
Joseph & Leah Garmai Taylor

Deb Akande
Lula Allen
Freya Bomba
Loida Bonney
Bill Carroll
Liz Cooke
Derresa Davis-Tobin
Vivian Garber
Doris Kelly
Elizabeth Leonard Clifton

Acknowledgments

Barbara Lindsey

May Mamiya

Kelly Mascetta

Carmen McGill

Lucette Mésinèle

Grace A. Ogana

Clara Rivera-Keita

Dain Rogers

Al Stevens

Robert Wright

Lynda Youmans

Denise Zahakos

Ophelia Amegashie

Veronica Anyango

Andrea E. Clarke

Joe Connell

Louis and Patricia Connell

Maureen Crush

George Danko

Gabriella Drasny

Courtenay Escoffery

Maria Elena Ferrer Paredes

Russel & Teren Gomez

Yvette Irvin

Jenny Jean Jerome

Nicola King

Delores Maragh

Mark Maragh

Nicola Maragh

Steven Maragh

Yvette McIntosh

Belinda Passafaro

Erica Salzmann-Talbi

Stephen Speziale

Keith Tombrello

Jennifer Trujillo

Darnell & Celia White

Claudine-Lonje A. Williams

Jennifer Hafner

Mirtha Miro

Louis & Louann Provenzano

Jocelyn Schur

Lorna Toby

Roseanna Valerioti

In Gratitude

The Liberia Project was the idea of my husband, Joseph Taylor. Thank you for your generous spirit, vision, and patience.

This project happened as a result of the following donors. Thank you:

Debbie Akande

Lula Allen

Veronica Anyango

Nichola & Dwight Archer

Arlington HS Student Club

Rodrick Armstrong

Laurene Bengel

Margaret Bennermon

Curtis Boddie

Freya Bomba

Hortense & Melmuth Brissett

Diane Browne-Sterdt & Philip Sterdt

Orlanda Brugnola

Fabiola Buddan

Eric Buergers

Lynn & Doug Cannon

Gerald Charleston

Janice Clarke

Andrea Clarke Hanson

Elizabeth & Alan Clifton

Dale Corzine

Maureen Creagan

Dawn & Minerva David

Angela Davis

Jobsaurie (JB) Decena

Desmond Dederick

Mayte and Reinaldo DeJesus

Donna Dorrier

Debbie Dunn

Kathleen Durham

East New York SDA Church

Paul Falchert

Jean Fox

Doxie Ferguson

Adanna & John Franklin

Kathleen & Dave Fuller

Felicia Gambles Kollie

Neil Geiselhart

Genesis SDA Church

Gloria Gibbs

Jalen Gilliam

Joe-Lynn Ginese

Jackie Goffe-McNish

Beverley Gohagen

Mrs. Golden

Elizabeth Handman

Kim & Jon Handman

Rachel Handman

Antoine Hanson

Rosane & Ben Hayes

Millicent Hayles

Gwen Higgins

Sue & John Hoctor

Marcine Humphrey

Judy & Joseph Iacovino

Ursus Idosu

Yvette & Philip Irvin

Alice Jalloh

Anna & Jerry Jamel

Jean & Jenny Jerome

Noreen & Kenwick Johnson

Denise Kellerhouse

Stephanie King

Cathy Kinn

Cary Kruzansky

Cyndi Landman

Mae Lawson

Bergie & Michael Lebovitch

Barbara Lindsey

Courtney Lynch

Ann Maguire & Dean Poorman

David Mahoney

Pat Malin

Cora Mallory Davis

May & Lawrence Mamiya

Delores Maragh

Jennifer Marino

Kathy McClain

Kaye Merrihew

Annette Mobley

Joan Monk

Loida & Eugene Mooring

Marilyn Mundy

Annet Nakamya

Norma Nelson Dwyer

Grantley Nicholas

Margaret Nijhuis

Inez & Ruth Niles

Obie Nsereko

Ilene & Terry Osbourne

Belinda Passafaro

Marcine Patrick

Kathy Peifer

Angela & Emerson Piercy

Louann & Louis Provenzano

Sylvia Ray

Ravi and Sand Reddy

Kris Revelle

Christine Rinaldi

Clara Rivera-Keita

Lorraine Roberts

Dane & Lester Rogers

Evelyn Rogers

Mary & Richard Rorie

Joyce Rotas

Cathy Rubino

Christi Sablinski

Cerena Scipio

Zina & Joseph Sesay

Therese Sibon

Ruth & Clinton Simmons

Loretta Spence

Sarah Stern & Rene Leon

Mary B. Summerlin

Marie Tarver

Helen Tester

Lorna Thompson

Lorna & Jose Toby

Michelle Tombrello

Jennifer Triplett & Michael Courtney

Carmen Tyrell

Robert Valeris

Thelma & Charles Valerus

Pat Webb

Janice & Paul Weir

Sherre Wesley

Maria Whalen

Celia White

Robert Wright

Marjorie Young

Introduction

I'm brought to laughter and joyful tears when I reflect on my experience or read over my journals that document my husband's and my travels to West Africa. During the summer of 2010, Joseph and I had the most thrilling experience of constructing a building that now functions as a church and school in Zorzor, Liberia. We chose Zorzor, or perhaps I should say Zorzor chose us. Joseph, who is from Liberia, had visited his grandmother in Zorzor two years earlier—just before she died at 103 years old. After completing his college years in America, he had not been able to return to his homeland because of prolonged civil wars. Liberia is still recovering from the lingering effects of war, an estimated 200,000 people are reported to have been killed and the country's economy devastated.

After his three-week visit to Monrovia, the capital, and then to his grandmother's home in Zorzor, the rural interior, he returned with a commitment to actively do something to help the people there. He promised the community, who had taken care of his grandmother during and after the civil wars, that he would assist them in some way. Within a few months, he completed several bike rides—including a 100-mile ride—to raise funds. Adding from our own savings, we had enough money—$500—to send to the people so they could buy land and construct a church there, which is what the group said they needed. The newly-constructed church would replace the dilapidated mud hut they had been using.

After some probing into the educational system, I suggested to Joseph that he inquire about the possibility of including a school in their plans. Readily, they welcomed that prospect. Once they had the land we realized, however, there were still not enough resources for them to reach their goal. We decided to set up a special savings account and accumulate funds that would help them build the church and school. Our excitement spilled over to others in our circles—family, friends, co-workers— and they began to donate to our cause. As the money donated by them increased, we felt a responsibility to be accountable and make sure the funds were spent as planned. We made a pledge to actively take part in the work. When we bought our plane tickets, a wave of excitement at this undertaking took over and our commitment to this project was sealed.

For three weeks, we left the comforts of home to do what we could to help. We were not an organization, just two individuals—supported by others—who saw a need and decided to meet it. Our hope was to positively impact a group of people, potentially, an entire community. And what a transforming experience it was for us! Our lives have been forever changed, and the experience is ever-present.

Moments from our time in Liberia flash across my mind when I'm ready to complain about some minor inconvenience, when I'm tempted to buy something that I quickly realize I don't really need or even want, or when I look at my baby girl and think of her coming into existence after our trip. Some say it was the result of living in the pure air and eating wonderful, fresh food; others say I recognized in the people and came to accept in myself the value of having children of one's own, no matter what our life circumstances; and, still, there are those who say God blessed our gift of service to our brothers and sisters on the other side of the world. Perhaps, it's all of the above.

Our hair textures were similar and our skin colors reflected the same shades of brown as theirs, but to the people of Zorzor, Joseph and I were the noteworthy ones to be celebrated. After all, we had come all the way across the world to assist them—Joseph returning to his home and I accompanying him—to make good on his promise to help. Yet, in the end, it was clear that they were the ones to be admired— the generosity they showed us; the work ethic they exhibited; the determination they maintained in circumstances that would be unfathomable to some. Indeed, being under this part of the sky, Zorzor, was an unforgettable experience.

And the journey begins...

Chapter One

We were exhausted and hot, having traveled from New York to Belgium, stopping at the Ivory Coast, and finally arriving in Monrovia, Liberia. Linda, our sister-in-law, and Seplu, a relative, arrived at the airport in an SUV to pick us up. Reginald, Joseph's brother, had to work late and planned to meet us at their home. I was surprised and a little disappointed, I'm embarrassed to say, by both their mode of transportation and their appearance.

Beaming with the brightest of smiles, Linda looked like any other brown-skinned woman I might see in an American airport. Dressed in a blouse and jeans, she greeted us with kisses on each cheek and full-body hugs. When she turned to direct us to the vehicle, her long braids dangled down her back—the honey-colored highlights standing out and adding to her attractiveness. Seplu—also dressed in a t-shirt, jeans, and sneakers—greeted us in the same manner. He deposited our suitcases in the car and then jumped into the driver's seat. Joseph and I got in the back of the white SUV and settled into the beige leather seats. *You know better*, I thought to myself.

I was very aware of the false image often conveyed about people in Africa, Asia, and other developing countries—a sense that the people are so far behind the rest of the world in almost everything. Once, someone even asked Joseph if people wore shoes in Liberia. He just laughed. Yet, there I was, let down by the very western and not atypical look of the people. I wanted an authentic experience and wondered if we were being treated to something other than how they normally lived. I was very aware of how people can go out of their way to make others feel welcomed, and I hated the thought of Joseph's family putting themselves out—spending money on things they couldn't afford—for our benefit. On the other hand, while surprised by some of the more modern components of his brother's house, I must admit that I had no qualms about enjoying them. I was very grateful and quite honestly a little bit relieved.

Our Arrival – Activities of Daily Living

Wednesday, 6/30

Joseph had prepared me for the many differences in privileges that I would find in Liberia as compared to our daily living in New York, and western countries in general. He made clear, though, that some of those major differences came after the wars; the destruction had definitely set his homeland back by years. So it was with a happy heart—and a sigh of relief—that we made our way through his brother's house in Monrovia to the room offered to us and the bathroom within. This bathroom appeared to be only slightly less modern than what I was used to.

Like the rest of the house, though, there were concrete floors and walls. It was also hot. "It is rainy season," Linda reminded me; perhaps she saw me pulling on my shirt collar and blowing air downward. However, more importantly, the basics of a bathroom were present. There was a toilet, one of my biggest concerns given Joseph's stories about outhouses, bushes, and the like. To my pleasant surprise, there was even a bathtub. I was definitely ready for a shower—to unwind and get out of the clothes I'd worn for almost twenty-four hours. Without realizing it, I must have said as much out loud.

"No, there is no shower," Linda seemed concerned.

"Oh, that's okay, no problem," I replied.

"You are ready for a bath?" Linda and I were meeting for the first time and she was eager to please, to make us feel at home—as I would later experience with other Liberians; indeed a warm and welcoming people. "You need hot water? I will heat it for you."

"Oh no, you don't have to do that." Linda had already taken my bags, brought house slippers to me, and referred to the meal she had prepared—an experiment for her to cook vegetarian food. I certainly didn't want her to go and draw a bath for me too.

"No, no, I will do it."

"Sister, it will be cold."

"That's no problem," I continued, "if it is, I will just add a little warm water then."

"So…I should warm the water?" Linda looked at me with a little confusion on her face.

"No, it's okay," I repeated. Going into the bathroom and reaching for the faucet, I realized there was none.

"Ah…Joseph," I called out as softly as I could. "How do I turn on the water?"

True to form, he laughed. "Remember, I told

you…there's no running water here anymore. You have to use the water in the barrel."

I turned around to see the large barrel filled with water. Now, I understood Linda's perplexed look. Okay, I thought, as I stepped out of the tub. I refused to let it be a problem. Before embarking on our journey, I had determined not to complain. It was my choice to come, and I wanted to see the project through. I put my finger in the water to check the temperature and realized why Linda had asked me if she should warm it. The chilliness of the water would be a bit of a shock to my body initially but refreshing after the day's journey. I was still a little confused.

"Hmm…sweetheart," I whispered to Joseph again, "one more thing…how exactly do I get in?" The barrel was a little more than waist high and though I considered various possibilities, I couldn't quite figure out how to climb in without the risk of creating a scene, which would bring my very eager-to-help in-laws and all the children running into the bathroom.

Joseph laughed again before finally responding. "You see that smaller bucket in the tub?"

"Yes," I responded hesitantly.

"That's your bucket. The barrel is for everyone. Take water with the pitcher that's in the barrel and empty it into the bucket and use that. Do the same if you have to use the toilet—pour the water in to flush."

Of course, I immediately looked at the toilet. Yes, indeed, there was nothing with which to flush. After some back-and-forth chatter, I emptied a few pitchers of water into the bucket in the tub. Then, I stood in the bucket. The water reached below my knees. I couldn't help but look over at the barrel. Had I gotten in it and crouched down a little, the water might have reached my chin—which was just what I needed. I must have made some sounds that drew Joseph in.

With a smirk and a sly smile, as if to mock me, he said, "Don't stand in the bucket. Here…" Joseph continued to instruct me while he held my hand to help me step out of the bucket and into the tub. He squeezed some soap gel on the wash cloth, both of which were new with the tags still on them.

"After you're done, use this cup," he took a large plastic cup from the sink counter and put it in the bucket, "to rinse yourself."

"Oh…" I smiled, uncertain about why all that hadn't initially come to my mind. "Got it."

I used my hands to rinse my face, and though the water was cool, it felt refreshing. However, when I started to pour a cup of water over my body to rinse, and although I tried to contain myself, I let out a scream.

"Oh, mama!"

Immediately, I heard Linda. "Sister, you need help?"

"Please make sure that door is locked," I quickly said to Joseph in a hushed voice. Shivering, I was frozen in one spot. There was a cloth hanging in the doorway between the bathroom and the bedroom where Joseph was standing. A door hung between the bedroom and the rest of the house. I had heard voices from a few people who'd walked in and out of the bedroom, apparently wanting to offer us helpful tips. With no shower curtain to hide behind and only a thin cloth in the doorway, I didn't want anyone to walk in and see me.

"We're fine," Joseph called back to Linda.

Already fully aware of her desire to assist, I clenched my teeth and quickly doused myself with several cups of water. I grabbed the towel just in time to wrap myself when I heard Linda's voice and looked up to see her silhouette behind the cloth.

"Let me warm the water."

"I'm done."

"Sister, you are braver than me. I must warm my water. It's too cold for me." As she walked away, I heard her say, "Brother Joe, your water will soon be ready."

I stuck my head out. "You're having water warmed for you?" I asked with a hint of judgment and incredulity in my voice.

"Yes," he said, barely taking his eyes off the camera he was fiddling with, "that water is cold."

A Feast for Two

It was late, after midnight by that time, and the children—two nieces and one nephew—had been asleep. However, when we walked out of our room, Reggie, the seven-year-old, was waiting at the door.

"See, this is for you," he pointed to the table. The house was dimly lit. I learned later that the buzzing noise I heard was a generator that kept the lights on. I could see that the table was set for two—two plates, glasses, forks, knives, spoons, and napkins.

I heard scurrying and turned just in time to see Vie, the four-year-old, coming toward me. "Auntie… for you," she said as she held my hand and pulled me through the living room area and into the dining room section while her brother reached for the cover of a large dish in the center of the table.

"Okay…go and sit," Linda said to her children and took the cover in hand.

"Brother Joe, I try…no meat, cassava leaf with small palm oil and rice." I also saw some slices of avocado around the edge of the platter. "No meat," she said once more, smiling and shrugging her shoulders.

"I'm sure it's delicious…" I barely got the words out before Vie plopped into my lap as I sat down at the table.

"Okay, okay…give the woman a chance," another voice said.

"It's okay," I responded, hugging Vie close.

"Back to bed now before your sister wake up," Sunnyboy gently insisted and pulled them away. Sunnyboy—as he was called—was a caretaker of sorts. He watched over the children, washed dishes, ironed clothes, and provided extra security at night when Reginald worked late. In exchange, he had a place to live and his living expenses and university tuition paid. Later, I would find out that this was a common arrangement; less fortunate young people, mostly from the country, lived with extended family or friends for such an exchange.

After Sunnyboy left the room with the children, Linda went to tidy up the outer area—the kitchen area—with promises that Reginald would be home soon. Joseph and I were left to eat alone. Exhausted and not having much, if any, energy to hold a conversation, we were both grateful for this quiet time by ourselves. In fact, I don't even remember us exchanging any words with each other. However, I do remember that the food was delightful. The cassava leaf—a green leafy vegetable like kale or spinach—was well-seasoned with the palm oil fragrance that I had come to know from Joseph's and his mother's cooking. There were also avocado slices, my favorite, and slices of roasted breadfruit—another treat for me. The spread was abundant. We didn't even eat half of what had been put out for us, and I knew they had gone above and beyond to provide us with such a wonderful feast.

That night, with the breeze blowing the sheer curtains to and fro, feeling refreshed from a cool bath, satisfied by a good meal, and nestled under the mosquito net put up for us, I felt the thrill of the possibilities to come.

Chapter Two

Monrovia is a paradoxical city—high-rise buildings and professionals in business attire interwoven with war-torn devastation, men with amputated limbs, burnt-down structures, and UN peacekeeping forces. Embarrassingly, I hadn't thought of Liberia in the former way and was again ill at ease with my surprising ignorance. I had expected village living of sorts—small towns or farms with only a handful of people. I did not expect the hustle and bustle that could have been Wall Street. Nor did I expect the island-like palm trees, an inviting Atlantic Ocean, or carefree boys playing soccer on the sandy beach.

Except for the remnants of war, Monrovia could have been any thriving metropolitan capital or vacation paradise. Unfortunately, we had limited time there, spending only a couple of days to gather the supplies we needed for construction of the church and school in Zorzor. Otherwise, had we stayed longer, I would have visited the Executive Mansion and The Temple of Justice on Capitol Hill—so prominently were they featured in the book I was currently reading, *This Child Will Be Great*, by Liberia's president, Ellen Johnson Sirleaf. I would have also stopped at the university, always drawn to campuses wherever I visit. Certainly, I would have made additional trips to the beach; we only visited it once after we returned from the work in Zorzor.

The Road Traveled – Going from Monrovia to Zorzor

Friday, 7/2

Our ride through parts of Monrovia was slow, as the streets were crowded. At Waterside, a marketplace just outside the city, every street was packed with people selling a variety of merchandise—fish, coconuts, used clothes, bed sheets, cell phones, and much more. In addition, there was competition between the cars and motorcycles; there were plenty of the latter. Both transported people and goods throughout the city and outskirts. The drivers raced down the same packed streets and went dangerously fast.

No one seemed distracted by the constant noise of horns or shouts of warning to pedestrians and approaching vehicles. Stop-and-go traffic nearly running over bystanders is not a foreign concept to me. I am a New Yorker, after all. However, in New York, one experiences the consistent presence and observation of traffic lights, on-duty police who direct traffic in busy areas, pedestrians who mostly stay on the sidewalks, and riders donned with bike helmets. All offer some reassurance of safety. As we raced through the jam-packed streets of Monrovia, I had no sense of protection.

At one point, my attention was drawn to a woman carrying a basket on her head that contained way too many jelly coconuts—the young version of the fruit where the inside flesh can easily be scooped out and eaten. The woman was older—her silvery hair and slower gait alongside our car made that clear—however, her rich chocolate skin was flawless and taut and didn't betray her age. At Joseph's request, Collie—the driver hired to take us to Zorzor—stopped for us to lighten her load by buying some of the coconuts. Then, a flood of sellers ran out in front and over to the passenger's side to show us their goods. Startled, I thought for sure we had run over someone, maybe even the old lady. I gasped. In a flash, there were hands and voices petitioning for a sale. I breathed easy when I saw a slender arm stretch through the window with a coconut, and soon after, her brilliant smile appeared as well.

"They are used to this," Collie said, acknowledging my concern. "They are quick. Even she…"

"How many?" she asked Joseph. She had already pulled out her machete to chop off the tops so we could drink the water and scoop out the jelly inside.

Joseph exited the car and held out his hand. "Let me…" He took six coconuts, depositing them in the back seat next to me. Then, he sliced off the tops of another three for each of us.

When he handed her the money, much more than she was expecting as payment for the coconuts, she held his hands between hers. "Tank you," poured out of her mouth and her eyes too. With nothing left in the basket, she held it under her arm and waved to us as we continued on our way.

"What are we going to do with all these?" I asked, emptying the liquid from my coconut while trying to keep my eyes on the road.

"I don't know, but imagine how heavy all those are...and at her age?" Joseph simply replied.

Leaving Monrovia and heading to the country, the rural area, made the contrast between our countries even more apparent. Most of the streets in Monrovia and just outside the city are paved, Victor, Joseph's uncle, told me when we picked him up. He came along as a guide of sorts. Living between Monrovia and Zorzor, he insisted that he would be better at negotiating whatever was needed during our trip up country. He'd make everything go more smoothly, he reassured us.

Leaving the city and going too many miles per hour for road conditions, I didn't feel anything resembling smooth sailing. Once we hit the unpaved roads, our drive got even worse. Uncle Victor turned around more than once to remind me that he had told me so. Potholes in New York City have nothing over the dusty, rocky roads—separated by chasms—on which we drove. It was the bumpiest ride I had ever taken, and I held on for dear life—sometimes to the door handle, at other times to Joseph, and frequently to both.

Still, Collie didn't slow down. At first, I attributed the speed to his youth. However, I was mistaken about his age—initially I asked if he was allowed to drive since he looked like he was in his late teens. It turned out he was actually in his late twenties. Someone really needs to bottle what maintains the Liberian youthful appearance! Driving as if in a race, over huge rocks in the streets, craters that split the land, and some muddy roads, he was completely unaffected by the hurdles. In the end, that caused us more delay than if he'd simply driven more slowly.

What should have taken a few hours to travel took us much longer. To be exact, it was eight hours filled with a few unpleasant quests because "nature called," a bump on the head which almost left me unconscious—the result of running into bamboo as I fled from a lizard in hot pursuit of me—and three flat tires. The last "bump" in the road took out two tires at once, and we were forced to pull over with nothing but a prayer. We just happened to stop in front of a mechanic. By that I mean a man who sat under a palm tree hut, with rubber hanging from the branches that held up the structure, and a generator attached to something that produced air.

After inviting us under his hut to sit in the shade, he went to work. He proceeded to patch the tires— pulling out the rocks that were stuck and rubbing rubber into the places where the rocks had been. Moving closer, Joseph hovered over the mechanic's shoulder. He looked back at me in both disbelief and admiration.

"Can you believe this? He's patching the tire with practically no tools."

No, I couldn't believe it. Just as I couldn't believe how fast the driver had been going, how *not* drivable the roads were, and how many hours had passed since our journey began and I'd had my last meal or drink. I was desperately trying to avoid the need to use the bathroom again.

Nature Calls

The first time I "had to go" was after we stopped in a little town. As we walked along the dusty road, we encountered a few people scattered about in front of their shops, with even more people gathered in the central market area. We seemed to draw the attention of all—some people smiled while others just followed us with their eyes; even the meandering dogs fixed their gaze on us. The people looked like they were from another time; not at all like the Monrovia crowd we'd experienced a few hours earlier. It was obvious that we were no longer in the city. There were one-room bungalows as well as thatch and mud huts. The residents walked down the road at a much slower pace than the "city dwellers" of Monrovia. In this small town, the people also wore more traditional clothing—African shirts and blouses along with lappas—the cloth women used as a dress, skirt, baby carrier, and more.

Uncle Victor said we could get a better deal on rice and oil in this small town rather than in the city, so upon our arrival he took to bargaining with Joseph close behind. I found out that this was Collie's hometown—along the way he greeted people he obviously knew. A young-looking man approached and greeted him with a full-body hug. My passing comment that they resembled each other made them both laugh, and they acknowledged that they were brothers. I was tickled by their affection for one another; until our departure they walked holding hands.

Since we were in the town that Collie called home, I asked if there was a bathroom around. Uncle Victor immediately responded affirmatively and walked me over to a shopkeeper he knew. I was relieved as he led the way with such confidence, since Joseph had responded with an "I don't think so" when I asked. After greeting each other, the shopkeeper nodded and we followed him. He unlocked a padlock on a chained fence; it was the backyard of his shop. As we proceeded inside, he unlocked another lock on a zinc door and beckoned me over. Joseph told me to wait and went first, pulling the door with his handkerchief and looking in.

"Got some tissues with you?" he asked, looking back at me.

"Yes," I confirmed with a smile. Even in much better circumstances, I had learned to be prepared. During a trip in Argentina, for instance, we got into the bathroom for free but had to pay for tissue squares. In Germany, we had to pay to get into the bathroom but the tissue was free, though limited. In the United States, we didn't have to pay for either, but sometimes neither was present.

"You should roll up your pant legs."

I figured that was code for "It's a bit untidy," so I obliged without question.

"I'll be right here," Joseph said. I was certain this was my husband's way of reassuring me that even though Uncle Victor and the shopkeeper were steps away, he would be guarding the door. And he had beaten me to it with his offer—it was the next thing I had turned around to ask of him.

When I stepped inside, I took some time to look around. The ceiling was the sky. The "bathroom" was a simple rectangular space with zinc at both sides. The walls of the adjoining buildings made up the longer sides. There were lots of little rocks on the ground and the "room" reeked of urine. I tiptoed a little here and there looking for a place to use the bathroom—I knew not to hope for a toilet, *but shouldn't there be a pit, a hole, something noticeable?* I questioned. Alas, there was not. I understood that time was passing and could hear the men just outside talking. I knew they were waiting for me, aware of what I was doing, or at least what I'd intended to do. I moved toward the door with plans to just hold it but remembered that for hours during our drive I had not seen anything but bushes. My mantra came back to mind: *I will not complain. At least there is privacy,* I thought, as I made my mark on the rocks—and, sadly, on my pants as well.

The second time nature called was a few hours later when we stopped to investigate a flat tire. I had to go in the bushes off the side of the road. Needing to go earlier, when we had stopped in Banga, I had declined because of the "feel" of the place.

Banga is a major town along the road from Monrovia; it's a crossroads of sorts, as people diverge to various places from there. Though still no Monrovia, it boasted more people than I had seen thus far along the way—with lots of shops and folks waiting around outside. There were also large gatherings of young men on motorbikes who apparently used their vehicles as taxis. I learned that the people milled about and negotiated transportation with the "taxis" so they could continue on their journeys. At one point, I noticed a man who approached and collected money from the drivers. Rather than work for themselves, I found out later that the men on motorbikes often worked for someone else. The business and busyness of Banga made me decide to wait for another bathroom break; there just seemed to be too many people moving about, and I was afraid of people knowing, watching, and having to wait for me.

At first, I thought it would be a better situation to go off into the bushes. I wouldn't have the pressure of everyone knowing what I was doing as they waited outside. So while they fiddled with the tire, I went off on my own armed with my tissue and antibacterial gel. I walked far enough away from the road to not risk anyone seeing me as they drove or walked by. Although there was much less congestion than in the city, we did periodically see another car on the road or people on foot as they made their way from one town to the next.

Of course, I was also on the lookout for any critters that might come crawling my way. Almost done, I felt a sensation on my ankle and was immediately annoyed with myself, thinking I had done it again— wet my pants. *This is why the women out here wear lappas*, I thought. However, when I looked down, there were spots of blood on my ankle. This sent panic through me and I moved quickly. I didn't want to draw too much attention to myself, though, so I consciously chose not to run.

"Joseph…can you come here for a minute?" I called out. I was pointing down at my ankle when he came over.

"What happened?" he asked as he bent down to take a closer look.

"I don't know. Do you think something bit me?" I started to imagine all sorts of poisonous creatures that might have sunk their teeth into my ankle. The yellow fever vaccine and malaria pills I had to take in order to get a visa for Liberia wouldn't necessarily protect me against the various possibilities.

"Blade grass," Uncle Victor was bent down too and identified the welts left on my ankle. Then he stood up and pointed to the bushes I had walked through. "It's sharp."

Joseph poured some water over my ankle and then

put some of the antibacterial gel on his handkerchief and wiped it down.

"When we get to Zorzor, we'll put some charcoal on it," he said, stroking my back. "At least it's not some poisonous bite," he smirked as we walked back to the car. He knew me too well.

The third bathroom trip was on the grounds of a medical clinic. I was encouraged when we stopped, observing this structure as more sturdy than anything I'd seen throughout our road trip thus far. The village didn't have much going on, though, and I barely saw anyone other than the clinic manager and a helper. They explained that they were located at a midpoint where local people could more easily get to them from either direction. There were several cots inside and some basic medicines. They also had a doctor and a nurse who stopped in monthly along with transportation in case they needed to get someone more urgent aid. Joseph engaged them in further conversation by asking about their funding and the common complaints of the people who came to the clinic. I found myself going in and out of the conversation, distracted by whether or not they might have a bathroom I could use. *There must be*, I thought. I assumed that because of the building's appearance—it was a clean-looking clinic made of concrete—there had to be genuine bathroom facilities on site.

"Hey, while we're talking, is there someplace my wife can use the bathroom?" I heard Joseph ask.

Nice job, hubby, I thought.

"Yes, in the back. Come," the clinic manager cheerfully signaled.

I felt some relief when I saw the outhouse—a structure with a door that was even painted blue and white. When I opened the door I noticed the plug—a piece of wood with a long handle—over the pit. When I closed the door, it was fairly dark. I was glad for the rays of light from the air holes and cracks along the structure. As soon as I moved the plug to the side, something dashed out. There was no mistaking it— something was in there with me. I jumped, threw the plug back over the hole—I think—held tight to my pants and took off. In a hurry, I forgot to duck and bumped my head on the low doorway as I fled. Once outside, I stood still only long enough to rub the sore spot on my head and then saw it. A dark green lizard, almost equal in size to my foot, came through the door and was fast approaching my heels. The sight of it jolted me into a run again and though I surely felt the impact, I didn't see the bamboo stalks in front of me. I did see stars and heard a ringing in my ears after I hit them.

"Oh God, please let me zip up my pants before I pass out," I heard myself say out loud.

"Everything okay?" Joseph and the clinic supervisor were walking back from the other side of the building. "Wait there one minute," he called out as he aimed his camera at me.

"LIZARD!" I screamed and ran toward them.

This caused a great deal of laughter from the clinic supervisor and the helper—but not from me.

It was after those events that we stopped to deal with the two flat tires and the mechanic under a palm tree hut. Limping about, I tried to ignore how the stinging from my swollen ankle had intensified. Nursing the bump on my head, I flashed a less-than-sincere smile in response to Joseph's wonder at the work of the mechanic. Still determined not to grumble, though, I turned away to take in the scene around me.

There were a few goats and some chickens walking about. Following them with my eyes, I noticed people staring at us from the mud huts across the dusty road. Steam billowed out from a pot poised over hot coals. This only added to my disorientation—for a moment everything seemed to be moving in slow motion behind the haze of steam.

The people too seemed confused by our presence. In fact, the children were frozen in their steps— looking over their shoulders, eyes fixed on us, they stood with buckets on their heads. They seemed taken off guard by our existence. I waved and smiled—my attempt to break their trance and ground myself. The smallest of them, who couldn't have been more than ten years old, immediately flashed her ivory teeth. In contrast to her coffee-colored skin and the red basin on her head, the whiteness of her teeth created a stunning image. Instinctively, I reached for my camera to capture the scene but was hesitant about how the people might react. I wondered if taking their photo would be considered offensive. Unfortunately, my friendliness didn't thaw the others; the three older children continued to look puzzled. I felt uneasy.

Perhaps it was their continued staring—even the adults hadn't shifted their positions—which contributed to the feeling that there was no light at the end of this tunnel. As I looked at the rough road ahead, fought the mounting urge to go to the bathroom, and tried to ignore the pain in my ankle and head, I thought, *We are really far away from home*. For the first time, I was apprehensive about what it would be like in Zorzor. It was only my third day in Liberia, and I was questioning my decision to have come.

Just then, a familiar sound I knew all too well brought my attention back to the mechanic. He put the rubber down and reached into his pocket. Pulling out a cell phone, he greeted the caller a few times— evidently, there was trouble with the connection.

"You can hear me, oh?" he finally screamed into the phone in true Liberian fashion, akin to Canadians ending their sentences with "eh."

I couldn't help but laugh out loud and was immediately relieved.

Chapter Three

My excitement and determination were rekindled when we finally arrived in Zorzor. I had fallen asleep and didn't see the crowd that had gathered, lining up along the side of the road as we entered the town. As soon as I exited the car—glad to stand and stretch, relieved to straighten out my constricted limbs and shake off the heat of the car—I took a quick glance around and smiled at those looking back. Quickly, I moved to help the others unload the supplies we'd brought—among them bags of rice, a small generator, a cooler, along with boxes of bottled water, sheets, and pillows to cushion our bodies on the mud hut floor where we expected to sleep.

Joseph's family interrupted our progress with enthusiastic welcome. Adults and children alike appeared and surrounded Joseph, holding on tight. When his Aunt Kayea came running out, we moved toward her, meeting her on the porch. After she embraced Joseph and her brother—Uncle Victor— and before either of them could utter a word, she turned to me. Looking up to the sky and stretching her hands above, she began to sing in her native tongue, Loma.

Safely in the Arms of Zorzor

I looked to Joseph, as now it was I who was frozen in my steps, a smile plastered on to hide my confusion and overwhelming discomfort with being the center of attention. Reading my thoughts, Joseph explained. "She is thanking God for bringing you here safely, to Zorzor, to her." I could see her teary eyes as she continued to sing and take unhurried steps toward me. My uneasiness vanished.

There have only been three times in my life when I felt so welcomed, when someone appeared overjoyed at my presence and reading it in their eyes left me, in turn, speechless. The first time was when my mother and I were reunited after being separated for about a year instead of the few weeks we'd expected. More recently, it happened when I entered a room and watched my seven-month-old daughter's gaze shift as I walked toward her and she recognized me—eyes lighting up, smile widening, with hands and feet flailing about so her father could hardly contain her. On this day, in Zorzor, Liberia, when Aunt Kayea sang a prayer of thanks to God for me, I was left awestruck. I felt her all-encompassing affection even though we were meeting for the very first time.

Aunt Kayea was in her late sixties; however, like the other Liberians I had met so far, I couldn't tell. Her caramel-colored skin was taut and her movement spry. With her petite body wrapped in a maroon print lappa, along with her head-tie that concealed her hair color, she certainly didn't look like she had yet passed mid-life. When she reached me, putting her forehead to mine, she said a few things in English—I'm told—and then hugged me close. My greeting of, "Hello, I'm Wendy," and "Thank you, that's so sweet," paled in comparison to hers. Then, she laid down a white cloth in front of the entrance to their mud hut. The singing began once more. She beckoned me, uttering a few words that again escaped me. Confused, I turned to Joseph.

"She wants you to walk on it," Uncle Victor exclaimed.

"No, no," I immediately said and tried to pull her up from her bent-over position. "My shoes are dirty." Besides the fact that I was horrified to put my dusty shoes on her bright white cloth, I again felt the discomfort of being the center of attention. It seemed to me that the whole town was watching this scene play out. However, Aunt Kayea wouldn't budge. In fact, she held my ankle and moved my foot forward onto the cloth, as if to show me what to do.

"She's not going to stop," Joseph finally said. "Just walk on the cloth until you get to the entrance."

Uncle Victor continued, "It is the way of welcoming you. She must do it, and you must let her."

And so I did. It didn't matter anymore that people were watching or that the cloth was becoming increasingly filthy. I was glad to honor her.

Some of those who came to greet us were looking forward to getting reacquainted with Joseph and talking with him in person. After having met when he visited his grandmother two years prior, they had kept in touch via periodic phone calls or messages through his brother to work out the building plans. Others who were also a part of this core group came to meet him for the very first time. Although this was my first contact with any of them, you would not have known it by their actions—everyone's greetings were extremely warm, sincere, and friendly, as if we were all reuniting after some time apart.

"Brother, Sister," one after the next said. "We cannot contain ourselves. We are happy."

When Joseph introduced me, I extended my hand for a handshake. They smiled at me, looked at each other, and chuckled a little. Perhaps they were taken off guard by my formal "American" gesture of greeting. Some followed suit—I imagine simply out of respect and to match what I had offered. Others, too full of enthusiasm to settle for such a reserved form of welcome, grasped both my hands in theirs and then pulled me close. Touching their cheeks to mine, they exclaimed, "You are welcome…we are happy for you." It was with such a delightful "culture shock" that our first evening in Zorzor passed.

The larger group left us for a little while to be alone with the family. Aunt Kayea, along with her daughter—who was nicknamed Old Lady but was *only* in her thirties—and Old Lady's daughter, Zizi, led the way off the porch and through the entrance to their home. It was more solid and larger than a typical mud hut, though still made out of a mix of mud blocks and straw. The entrance was a hallway that branched off into several different rooms, which were rented by other people. The hallway led to a backyard kitchen where others stood and greeted us with their smiles. Aunt Kayea, Old Lady, and Zizi scurried ahead, handing covered bowls to each other and directing us into a room. It was dark inside. Besides the light coming through the cracks in the mud, we could barely see, so we propped the door open initially. Aunt Kayea said something quick to Zizi and she appeared with a lantern; Joseph remembered buying it for his grandmother when he had been there previously. Shuffling around in his backpack, he took out a flashlight. There were two mattresses on the floor—which we were told had been bought by Joseph's mother during one of her visits—a pile of pots and bowls were stacked in one corner of the room and a host of large bags and several traditional outfits hung over a rope in another corner.

"Sit…" Aunt Kayea tapped the mattress and invited me over. "Junior, you here," she pointed to a stool on the other side of the table that now sat between us. Most of Joseph's family calls him Junior, as he was named after his father, a senator in Liberia who died during the wars.

Once Aunt Kayea sent Zizi out of the room to talk with her friends—a host of smiling children who stood at the doorway—she and Old Lady settled down on the other mattress across from us.

Old Lady explained, "Junior…palm butter, rice, and plantain," and smiled as she lifted the plates that covered the bowls of food.

"Oh, my favorites," Joseph responded.

"Yes, and no meat," Aunt Kayea assured us.

"Thank you," I responded. "Aren't you going to join us?"

"No, you eat," they said in unison. They were all smiles from the beginning of the meal to the end.

Having only one spoon on the table, I asked if there was a fork, which seemed to confuse them.

"A fork? No, there is no fork," Old Lady immediately stood up.

"Another spoon," Joseph clarified.

"You need another spoon?" Eager to oblige, Old Lady moved quickly as Aunt Kayea pointed in the direction of the additional utensil, as if her daughter was a visitor too. They both still seemed perplexed because I wanted my own utensil and we used the dish that had been covering the bowl as a separate plate for Joseph. He and I ate and I mostly listened as they caught up on each other's lives, the excitement of having us there punctuating their sentences. I'm not sure if it was because I was so hungry after limiting my food and fluid intake during our earlier journey or that the spread was not as plentiful as what we'd experienced in Monrovia, but we cleaned our plates. In fact, Old Lady took note of it.

"Sister, you eat good," she said as she started to clear the table.

I've never been bashful about having a healthy appetite and didn't hold back then either.

A knock at the door signaled a transition to the next part of our evening.

Bedell, one of the elders Joseph had been communicating with during the past two years, had made arrangements for where we would stay. "Madame Sirleaf," Bedell explained, referring to the President of Liberia, Ellen Johnson Sirleaf, "gives money to women in the interior so they can have businesses. The woman, Mrs. Johnson, has a hotel nearby."

"A hotel?" I asked, surprised, curious, and definitely excited about the possibility of a shower and toilet.

"Yes, there is a van too!" Bedell matched my enthusiasm. "Only there is no money for gas or repairs, so it doesn't run."

When we made the walk down the street, we found our dwelling place was more motel-like than the hotel I had pictured in my mind. Still, it was a step up from the mud hut we'd expected. With a mattress on the floor, an indoor tiled area for a bath, and a toilet—buckets of water still required for both—we were thrilled and grateful.

After helping to carry our bags inside, the group of four or five who had greeted us earlier waited for us outside our room. We gathered in the front-yard area, which was set back from the main street.

"You must be tired from your journey. The sun is setting and Sabbath will soon begin," Dennis, another of the elders with whom Joseph had also communicated, spoke to us.

With that, he led everyone into a circle. We held hands, prayed, and sang together:

"The day thou gavest, Lord, is ended.
The darkness falls at Thy behest.
To Thee our morning hymns ascended,
Thy praise shall hallow now our rest."

Acclimating to This New World

The next day was a bit of a blur. I was still tired from our travels to get to Zorzor and had not slept well that first night. Trying to be efficient, I was scant with my use of the bucket of water they brought us before we went to bed so we wouldn't run out overnight. Once in bed, I attempted to get accustomed to the various sounds of the night. It appeared as if people were talking right outside our window, only what they were saying was muffled beneath the buzz of the nearby generators. The owner of the lodging was also showing a movie in the front yard, powered by a generator that stopped working somewhere before the end of the film. There had been plenty of uproar about that, I found out the next day when Mrs. Johnson apologized for the previous night's noise. There were also assorted barking dogs and every so often I was jarred awake by a group of passersby.

Apparently, Zorzor was a thoroughfare of sorts. People came to shop at its market and to find transportation to Banga as well as to other neighboring counties or even further to Monrovia. When I thought about it, the sounds weren't that different from some areas in New York. In fact, at one point I said, "It's like Grand Central Station out there." "No," Joseph replied, "Banga is Grand Central Station. Zorzor is the Metro North Station in Poughkeepsie."

Most especially, that first night I was concerned about mosquitoes. Joseph had been too tired to put the mosquito net up before we went to bed. In my opinion, he wasn't taking the matter seriously enough. I, on the other hand, didn't want to be forced to leave because I contracted malaria, nor did I want to have to navigate getting us back home if Joseph came down with it. Of course, he insisted that the mosquitoes were not interested in his Liberian blood—it was only the non-native blood they would be after. *More reason for me to be afraid,* I thought. So, I wrapped myself up from head to toe with the net, after I had lathered on insect repellent and sprayed the room. To make matters worse, I was worried I wouldn't be able to hear the mosquitoes approaching over all the noise outdoors. Needless to say, I didn't get much, if any, sleep.

I do remember that early the next morning about twenty to thirty people arrived at the mud hut church, the one we were about to replace with the new concrete building. Some came to worship, others wanted to thank us for coming to do the work, and a few were just curious. I can still hear the melodious singing—verses and entire songs in Loma, English, and French. During the war, many Liberians had taken refuge across the border in Guinea, which is about forty minutes by car. As a result, many of the people in Zorzor speak fluent French in addition to English and their native dialect. Though English is the official language of Liberia—and standard in Monrovia—there are many other languages spoken, especially further into the interior of the country.

By day's end, Joseph announced to the smaller group who had spent the day with us—as we sat on Aunt Kayea's porch, walked through the town, and visited the town's people—that we had limited time and needed to start working right away. He explained that we planned to be there for only ten days, just enough time to get the work off to a good start.

"We will tell the people to meet at the church— the mud hut—to discuss the plans," Dennis said as he bid us goodnight at our door.

"What time, Brother?" someone called out.

"Nine o'clock in the morning," Joseph looked at me to confirm and I shook my head.

"Yes…we begin tomorrow, at nine in the morning," one of the men echoed. With nodding heads and broad smiles, they eagerly agreed.

And so it was.

Chapter Four

We rose early the following morning—around 6:00 or 6:30 a.m., as we would do for the remainder of our time in Zorzor. Perhaps our early rising was because of the rest we'd had the day before or getting to bed earlier the previous night. Quite possibly, it was our excitement about going to the actual building site. It was certainly not because the noise had been any less—as in other places around the world, Saturday night brought out the party spirit in Zorzor too.

Wardrobe Woes

As I got dressed, I had some misgivings about my attire. I had already made peace with the fact that my clothes would be wrinkled. In Monrovia, we were told to put out our clothes the night before. By the next morning, Sunnyboy had taken care of them—they were starched, ironed, and hung on hangers ready for us to wear. In Zorzor, however, when I inquired about an iron I could use, Old Lady started to make plans. She intended to either have the seamstress in town heat the coals, put the iron on, and then bring the iron to Old Lady so she could iron my clothes or Old Lady herself would take my clothes to the seamstress. It all seemed a bit too much and not at all necessary. *Wrinkled clothes wouldn't kill anyone,* I thought, *and with the heat and perspiration and changing clothes a couple times a day, what was the point?*

My only remaining reservation was that I had packed only two skirts, which were more appropriate for church than for the day's plans. Expecting to be involved in manual work, I'd brought along what I thought would be best for that purpose—pants, cotton and linen long-sleeved shirts to give my skin a barrier against the sun, a wide-brim hat for the same reason, and steel-toed boots; Joseph insisted that if I was going to be on the site I should be safe. However, I soon realized how much wiser it was that the women wore skirts or lappas; it made it much more convenient for the bathroom-wherever-you-can-find-a-spot experience. At Aunt Kayea's there was a sectioned-off area in the back, much like the shopkeeper's in the town where we'd stopped on our way to Zorzor—privacy and lots of little rocks, but no pit. Elsewhere, there were just bushes. Nonetheless, I had to make do with the clothes I'd brought; though I planned to inquire about buying lappas as soon as possible.

Our walk just down the road to Aunt Kayea's for breakfast was filled with a mix of smiles, waves, and stares. Even with the partying the night before, people were up and already moving about. Old Lady and Zizi came out onto the porch to greet us, as one of the children had spotted us coming up the hill and announced our arrival. Aunt Kayea was already out running errands, getting the ingredients for our next meal. We had given her money to cover the cost of meals, and she took special care to seek out in-season treats for us—pineapples, jelly coconuts, and cucumbers.

"I should go find her for you?" Old Lady asked and began to dispatch Zizi for that purpose.

"No," Joseph responded, "We don't need her right now."

"Come…" Old Lady continued, "You ready to break your fast now?"

I laughed again, just as I had the day before when

she'd said it. She put her arm through mine, laughed, and then buried her head on my shoulder. "I say it wrong again."

"No, no," I insisted, leaning my head against hers. "It's just different, but it makes sense."

Once in the back, she took out two stools for us to sit on and uncovered a bowl that had been covered by another and wrapped with a cloth. It was rice with pieces of plantain and avocado. Zizi and several of the other kids—those belonging to the people who rented the other rooms and neighbors who had mud huts just behind—were off to the side sitting on the ground. They were preoccupied as they ate their rice and meat out of a community bowl. Old Lady talked with us from the kitchen—a palm-tree hut with a pit for cooking—while she continued to work on something. When we were finished and told her we had to get to the site, she took our bowl and asked if she should save the rest of the food for us for later. She had asked the same question the day before. After we responded, "No, we're done," she passed the remainder of the food to the children who welcomed it.

Old Lady said she would walk with us down the street. As was usual, Joseph held out his hand to help me off the porch since there were no steps. Someone walked over to him to introduce himself, so I held out my hand and helped Old Lady down from the porch. She was so overcome by the gesture that not only did she blush, but she wrapped her arms around my neck and said, "Oh Sister, I love you. I should help you." A neighbor called out something, which drew my attention to the fact that there were several people out on their porches observing us, all with wide grins. She said something back to them in Loma and leaned in closer to me.

Beginning the Work – Hard Labor

Sunday, 7/4

After talking with a group of about seven or eight at the mud hut, we decided it would be best to go directly to the building site to see what we were actually working with and to make our plans more practical. Instead of talking in general terms or having the location described to us and trying to envision the area, it made sense to be at the site to do the planning. We were told it was approximately three-quarters of a mile away and would take us about ten minutes to walk there.

As we proceeded to the site and turned off the road we took from the town, the men immediately warned us, "It is not really a road. It can be hard to walk, maybe for the woman..." one person said as they all looked at me. With the exception of me, only men were present.

"The woman is from New York," Joseph said under his breath, just loud enough that I could hear, as he held out his hand to help me over the bumpy ground. He was well aware that I wasn't going to miss any part of this experience and knew if anyone suggested it, I would insist that I was perfectly capable of handling whatever came my way.

"It's okay, don't worry about me. I'm fine," I felt a need to say to them, though thinking, *I'm already perspiring and I haven't started to do any work yet.* The ten-minute walk from the town to the mud hut was hilly, making the excursion a bit more challenging. On top of that, though early in the morning, the sun was already intense and gave off heat that made it feel like midday.

"You are ready to work, Sister," Mulbah joked, pointing to my boots.

"Yes, that's why I'm here...to work," I smiled back while paying close attention to every hurdle of rocks and branches over which I had to step.

About five minutes into our walk, they stopped to show us an area filled with concrete blocks. We had sent money in advance to have the blocks made ahead of time, knowing they would need time to dry in order to be ready for us to build with when we arrived.

"Oh, great!" Joseph exclaimed and then questioned, "But why are they here and not on the actual land?"

"No trucks or cars can go there. See," Dennis pointed behind and ahead of us, "this is not a road. We made this path." Apparently, the truck had dropped off the blocks on the road we took from the town to the mud hut and the people had had to move them one by one to their current location, which was still a distance from the building site.

"Now, we will move them closer to the site," continued Bedell.

With that said, each man picked up a block and began to walk. They motioned for us to come along. Not even thinking about whether or not I could manage it, I bent down to pick one up, but they told me not to. It was the beginning of our time together, so I decided to let them have it their way, for the moment anyway. Besides, I had no idea how much further I would have to walk. With perspiration already streaming down my back, I thought it best to heed their instruction.

I was sure glad I did. By the time we arrived at the actual building site, I was out of breath and the rice and plantain that Aunt Kayea made for our breakfast seemed a distant memory. Not only had it taken another ten minutes or so to get to our ultimate destination, but the scorching sun seemed to be melting me and the hike was one that required careful attention to prevent twisting an ankle or tripping over the uneven ground. Rather than a true road, it was indeed only a coarse path with bushes and branches jutting out at us. Sometimes we had to step aside to give the right of way to people carrying loads on their heads—buckets of water, basins with dishes, pieces of woods, and the like.

Oh my, was my first thought when we finally got to the site. I couldn't tell where we were supposed to start building. There were trees and shrubs everywhere. "We've been clearing the land," I heard someone say. All I could think was, *It was worse than this?* Since there were no large machines to clear the land or make a road for transporting the materials closer to the site, the men walked and used their machetes to go over every inch of the land.

A handful of men trailed Joseph and Anthony,

a local builder who was asked to head the work, as they surveyed the land. Within a half-hour of looking over everything, they decided there would be time and funds to put up one building for now, which would function as the church and provide classrooms in the back for the school. With Anthony's building expertise and Joseph's architectural background, they began drafting the plans.

The men used their feet, measuring tape, and cell phones—which everyone had, though most didn't have minutes to make calls—to calculate the widths, lengths, and number of cement blocks needed. Some of the men continued to clear the land with their cutlasses, while others went to find sticks and rope needed to outline where they would start digging the foundation.

And Then Came the Women...

Feeling a little out of place and having had enough of walking about, I was glad to see some women arrive. With cement blocks on their heads, they walked one behind the other just as the men had done during our walk to the site. The women varied both in physical attributes and in presentation. Some were tall while others were short; some had a solid build and others were thin; their skin colors ranged from caramel to toffee to dark-chocolate; even the clothing was wide-ranging—t-shirts, pants, native blouses, and lappas. Everyone carried the cement blocks.

As they approached me with smiles and greetings that made clear we had met the day before, I felt bad and just pretended to remember. I wasn't sure anyone would understand my drawn-out explanation about being so exhausted the day before that most things were a fog. Instead, I decided to make myself useful and join them on the trip back to get more blocks. During our walk, I heard "tank you" over and over. And though I was trying to pay attention to their appreciation, I was distracted—trying to decide whether or not I could actually carry the concrete blocks on my head like they did. In the end, I decided against it. After all the concern my mother had expressed about me getting malaria, yellow fever, or some other life-threatening malady, and whether the unrest that had led to the civil wars was really over— which had begun in the interior where we were—the last thing I wanted was for Joseph to have to explain to her how I broke my neck carrying cement blocks on my head.

So, I made two trips with blocks on my shoulders,

stopping along the way to rest and reassuring the women that I was fine. The blocks were extremely heavy, and the sun was blazing like a red-hot fire. I couldn't fathom how these women carried such a load and talked to each other with ease at the same time. As we approached the building site at the end of both trips, the men saw see me coming, abandoned their work, and ran over to help. Saying it was too much for me and that I was not used to such exertion, they encouraged me to take a break.

Joseph called out something about being careful and that maybe there were smaller blocks I could carry or some other way I might be of assistance. I ignored him. I am proud to say that I made the two trips carrying those blocks and reached our end destination without incident. Then, the last trip came.

Noticing my struggle during the other trips, a few women suggested it would be easier for me to carry the block on my head because it would be centered and cause less pain to my body the next day. Kolu, who was wearing pants underneath her lappa, took the lappa off and created a cushion out of it for the top of my head. It took three of them to get me ready. I bent down so Kloboh and Kolu could put the concrete block on top of the lappa cushion while Yamah held me in place.

I began to laugh and they followed suit, though I'm not sure we were laughing for the same reasons. I wished Joseph was nearby to take a picture or get this scene on video. *I'm not going to be able describe this,* I thought. Nor was I certain I would even believe it had ever happened. When I felt the weight of the concrete, I immediately held on with both hands as all three women guided me—with hands on my back and shoulders—to a straightened position. We all looked at each other and smiled. They hauled blocks on their heads and everyone proceeded forward.

"It feels just fine. You're right...much better than on the shoulders," I said at first. But after a few minutes of walking...no, it was probably more like seconds...and after taking just a few steps, I was ready to stop. My legs were beginning to buckle, my neck was trembling, and I was certain that my head would implode. So great was the weight that I felt a burning sensation from the top of my head to the bottom of my feet. I didn't take the block down, though. Quite frankly, I was afraid I wouldn't be able to get it off or back up again. There was also my pride. I stood off to the side and motioned for the ladies to go ahead.

"I'm okay...need to take a break. Don't want to slow you down, though." I could barely get the words out.

"No, we will not leave you. We will wait," Kolu smiled.

"Sister, I should take it for you," Kloboh started to reach for mine, which would have added to what she was already carrying. I couldn't let her do that.

"No, no. I'm ready now."

"You are sweating!" Yamah called out.

"Of course, I'm sweating!" I slowed down and called back, looking for a reason to pause once more. "I'm carrying a cement block on my head." The women laughed and then pointed to another who was making her way toward us with two blocks on her head.

"Show off!" I called out. This brought more laughter from the group and—thank God—it bought me more time to stand still.

Though I never took down the block, I prayed for strength the entire way. *Please God, don't let me fall. Don't let me break my neck. Please let me complete this last trip with this block on my head.* That kind of pride is a terrible thing. Feeling faint, the heaviness of the concrete causing a headache, perspiration dripping down my nose and lips, I stopped talking completely and uttered more silent prayers. I gave a whole new meaning to, "Pray without ceasing." It didn't fail me—I made it to the end.

Approaching the site, I saw a blur of several men, including Joseph, moving quickly toward me. Some were moving to take my load. Others were cheering me on. "Sister, you can work!" I heard someone call out. There were a few other comments, but nothing else registered.

I so desperately wanted to respond, "Of course, I can work" or, "I guess I inherited my mother's muscles." I even thought about the line I've often used to show my ability or lack of fear in other countries I've visited, "I'm a New Yorker, what do you expect?" But the truth was I didn't have the strength to utter even a single word. Once they helped me get the block off my head, I sunk down to the ground and drank my bottle of water in one fell swoop.

When I finally regained enough energy to look up, I was thrilled. In front of me was a well-cleared, roped-off area for the foundation of the building. On the ground close by me was the drafted plan of what it would look like. I could feel the muscles in my face again and managed to muster a smile. *Not too bad for a day's hard labor.*

Though I had vowed not to have anything to do with concrete again, the next morning we were back at the site and I was moving blocks once more. This time, though, I moved them in a wheel barrow. Anthony had brought it to the site and quietly pointed it out to me. Throughout our work together, he continued to gently direct me to more manageable ways to be involved. I was both glad and thankful for his insight. Yes, I was determined to help and wanted the people to know I wasn't just there to watch them work. However, I didn't have to pain myself to participate.

Chapter Five

At some point every day, rain poured down. Actually, each time it rained, we were grateful for the reprieve from the scorching sun and a cooling off of the red hot earth of Zorzor. Usually, though, the rain started and stopped early in the morning—before the crowing of the rooster, which caused the dogs to bark and somehow overlapped with the Muslims' start-of-the-day prayer song. It was truly a most wonderful way to be awakened—the singing that is. While I was in Zorzor, I had enough of both the crowing and the barking to last a lifetime.

A Usual Day

Normally, by 7:00 a.m., everyone was up and getting ready to work and only stopped when made to do so. This was often accomplished when I walked around the site and insisted that they take a break to drink the water I handed out. Every morning a cooler with bags of frozen water was brought to the building site. Joseph had negotiated prices with a woman in town, a shopkeeper, who filled plastic bags with water from one of the wells in town and kept them in a freezer powered by a generator. These frozen bags of water were the source of a good deal of business for her. It was also a lot more sanitary than the bucket of water and cup that initially had been shared by all at the site—after a few drinks the water was dirtied by the hands that were mixing cement, digging soil, and hauling blocks.

We also had to coax people to take a lunch break each day. Kloboh, to whom we gave a bag of rice and money so she could get the necessary goods from the market—including meat, fish, and beans—prepared rice and tobogi. Tobogi, like rice, is a staple. It is a sauce in which anything can be stewed. Each day when Kloboh arrived with her pots of sweet savors, I was continually astounded that no one seemed to notice. In order to get everyone to eat, Joseph, I, or one of the elders went around and called out for a food break. Finally, they would pause and have lunch in groups. Served in one big bowl for each group, the men, women, and children ate in circles among themselves.

I enjoyed this mealtime, as it was an opportunity for us to talk about something other than the building project. I got to hear about where they had been during the wars, what their plans were for school and life, and the myths they believed about America. They also asked questions of us. They wanted to know why I was so tall and where "my people" were from. Someone asked how many children we had and all eyes widened in disbelief when I said we didn't have children and might not want any.

Each day I taught the children of the village something new—how to spell our names or how to recite the alphabet, using a stick to draw letters in the dirt. The adults usually joined in, being just as curious and interested as the young ones. Somehow we'd end up in a group activity, laughing as they made fun of each other, taking turns to instruct me on the pronunciation of words in Loma, or joining in to pronounce my name. I watched each mouth contort itself to sound out the syllables and enunciate each letter as they traced the dirt etchings with their fingers.

I'm thankful we continued those moments in the evening on Aunt Kayea's porch because amidst laughter and in the middle of conversation during the day, the delight of getting the building up lured them all too quickly back to work. The breaks were indeed a brief activity; they were all counting the days until the church and school were built and ready to be used.

Everyone was excited beyond words and continued to show us gratitude. Without fail, Joseph and I were acknowledged and celebrated as we made our way around town. "We still cannot believe it," Dennis often said to us. "It is too much for our minds."

"You are welcome," people declared as they hailed us on the road with open arms, drawing us close and kissing us on both cheeks to complete the greeting. Others offered the "Liberian handshake," a snapping of fingers at the end of clasping hands. People even came from neighboring towns—walking miles to do their part of the work. "Tank you," we heard as we made our way through the market, stopped to pick up supplies, or went to the work site.

One evening, a Muslim neighbor of Aunt Kayea brought us a gift of half a goat. "It is blessed," he said.

We chose not to say we were vegetarians and shared it among Joseph's relatives. The children brought us cucumbers and other fruits or vegetables. "This is for you," Junior, a twelve-year-old boy said to me. "It is what you eat." The cucumbers, pineapples, and peanuts brought to us were yet another show of appreciation.

They were grateful that Joseph not only kept his promise to help, which he had made two years earlier, but that he had come back to be a tangible part of the aid and brought me with him. For that reason, Aunt Kayea named me "Garmai," which is Loma for "truth."

It was common for me to hear, "Garmai, I have something for you." Or, "This is for Garmai…to say tank you." In fact, one of the women, Mulbah's wife, gave birth during our first few days there. When we went to visit, we were introduced to baby "Wendy Garmai." Honored, I was speechless.

Rain, Rain, Go Away, Come Back Another Day — Not That It Matters

Tuesday, 7/6

On this particular morning, the rain was different.

It began during the night and had been raining for five hours straight. The rain hadn't stopped in time for us to go out and work at our usual early hour. In fact, that morning I couldn't hear if anyone else was up, so loud had been the pounding of rain for several hours. I was awakened by it at 2:30 a.m. I knew the precise time because I always slept with a watch and flashlight under my pillow in case I needed to identify some critter crawling on or biting me, which had happened one night.

At first, the rain came down like nails. Hitting the zinc roof on the houses of cement or mud, it made a rattle that might have lulled me back to sleep had I not become entangled in my mosquito net. I still used the mosquito net as a cover—the closer it was to my skin, the more protected I felt during the mosquito-swarming hours at dawn. Struggling to get free from the net, I was kept awake long enough to hear the clinking turn to thumping. The rain started to come down like sledge hammers pounding nails into the roof just above us. I had never heard or seen rain like this. "It's not raining cats and dogs," I later wrote on my faux postcards, "only lions and elephants." (Since no one in Zorzor or Monrovia had understood what I meant when I asked for postcards, I'd found a way to create my own, which I mailed from Monrovia.)

Around 9:00 a.m., when it finally let up, Joseph and I decided to make a run for it, hoping that the tapering off would soon come to a complete end. We were both anxious and eager, wanting to see as much of the building completed before it was time for us to return home. It was to our great surprise, and a testament to the people's hard work, that the construction was happening so quickly. In just a couple of days much had already been accomplished. It made us greedy for even more to be done in the eight days we had left. I was certain that everyone was as anxious as we were for the rain to stop. I knew they would be disappointed if our progress was drastically impeded; they were not only hoping to complete the building while we were there, but looking forward to all of us celebrating its completion together.

It was 9:30 a.m., and as we went further into town, Joseph and I saw that people were up and about. They were moving along as if there had been no downpour. Joseph looked up at the sky and said he thought the rain was done for now.

"So, you're able to read the sky now?" I said jokingly.

"I'm African…that's what we do," he said in his usual matter-of-fact way.

We began our trek to the site.

"At least it's a little cooler now," Joseph said.

"Yeah…so, how far behind do you think we are?" I was concerned that the rain had cost us too many hours of work. We had been counting the remaining days and identifying what still needed to be done, when materials would be delivered, how long things would take to dry before we could start the next phase, and whether or not we could spread the money until the end.

"I don't know," my always optimistic husband replied.

Anticipating the disappointment, I prayed the rain would stop so people could come out and work. Continuing to walk in silence, we waded through the muddy path to the site. When we arrived, men, women, and children were not only there, but already laboring—and it seemed they had been for hours. With our hearts warmed by their commitment, we joined in. Though the rain continued to slow us down periodically, it never stopped us.

Chapter Six

Every day, there were people who arrived to help with the building, walking miles from another town to get involved. They had heard about the work being done and wanted to join in. They came not knowing when their next meal would be or even where they would sleep. A day or two later, having contributed to the work, they took the journey on foot back to their homes.

This gave us opportunity for conversation with many Liberians from different counties "up country." As I learned more about Liberia—corruption of the leaders within, exploitation from the affluent without, fourteen years of bloodshed—I wanted to do much more for the people. I was moved to tears as I listened to the stories of how some survived, those families and friends who didn't, and the resulting devastation of the wars. Yet, these are a most resilient people—their radiant smiles, unrelenting courage, and overwhelming gratitude continue to inspire me.

The Aftermath of the Wars... The Resilience of the People

It wasn't uncommon to have people answer the questions I asked to get to know them better with, "Well, after the wars…" or "When the wars happened…" Some even referred to it as "World War I" or "World War II." I found those references odd, and when I finally asked after hearing them a few times, they began to make sense to me.

"Garmai, we had never experienced anything like that kind of massacre before."

"Our world came to an end when the wars happened."

"Sister, you didn't know if you would live or die…and sometimes, you prayed to die."

One man, a school friend of Joseph's, shared how he and his family were ordered out of their house one night and told to line up in the yard. They thought they would be killed. Instead, the torture they experienced went on day after day. Usually, the questioning revolved around whether or not they were involved with the rebellion against the current leader and which tribe their people were from. At other times, they were probed about insignificant matters. When I inquired, I often heard, as with this man and his family, how the rebels or soldiers—depending on whose point of view was taken—would play games with their victims. Some said it was a form of torture. Others said it was simply because those doing the questioning were boys—immature children who had been given power, weapons, and group protection. Fortunately, Joseph's friend and his family were not killed. However, they had lived for quite some time with the fear of death literally hanging over their heads.

One day as we headed back after picking up supplies, we saw a woman—with a heavy load of assorted goods on her head—walking down the road. Knowing that she could only be heading to Zorzor—there was no other destination for miles—we offered her a ride. During our conversation she touched on another issue that had crossed my mind.

"The Muslims and Christians live together now, but it is only a restless peace." She explained that everyone was still afraid because of the bloodshed that had taken place; they still found it hard to believe that neighbors and relatives could massacre each other in such a way.

I too had wondered about the relations between these two groups; in Zorzor there seemed to be a comfortable existence between Muslims and Christians. Neighbors and shopkeepers interacted with each other, and there was a certain respect as they allowed business to cease at specific times for daily prayers. In fact, Joseph was referred to a Muslim shopkeeper who graciously provided, on short notice, some of the materials we needed. "We serve the same God," was his response when Joseph thanked him. Given the news around the world about Muslims and Christians being at war in Africa and Asia, I was rather surprised to see their coexistence in Zorzor. I had also learned when I inquired in Monrovia that both sides had been subject to bloodbaths at the hands of the other during the wars.

The woman we picked up talked about how her brother's church had been burned to the ground and hundreds of people killed—not only the members of that congregation but also those who had sought refuge and been hiding there. When I asked how her brother handled it, she said, "He was burned too." Then she said, "We forgive because we must, otherwise it will happen again." Yes, I knew the importance of forgiveness; and yet, it seemed too great an expectation under the circumstances I continued to hear about. I realized too as I listened to this woman, how petty my few grudges with others seemed to be.

Another woman who came to sit with Aunt Kayea on the porch one day, shared how her sister "lost her mind" during the war. When the news spread through her town that "they were coming," this woman's sister hid her daughters in the well, "to save them from the violation the people said happened to the girls," she explained. The woman continued, "'They were crying,' my sister told me. My sister said she promised to get them soon, but told them they couldn't make any sounds. But they were young and frightened and someone told her after that the crying drew attention." With tears in her eyes, she revealed to me that none of the three little girls survived. As much as I wanted to know specifically what had happened, I also didn't. So, I didn't ask. Nonetheless, the knowledge of their story was stamped in my mind. That night I couldn't write in my journal. I couldn't even pray. Instead, I wept.

In addition to the heart-wrenching tragedies the wars reaped and Liberians experienced, there were other consequences just as long-lasting if not as severe. Education and pursuing one's goals were among those.

Edwin was one of the men who helped out a lot at the site and with whom I had many a conversation. I later found out that he was in his thirties—though again, I thought he was in his late teens or early twenties. Edwin shared how he and his family had escaped to Guinea when he was just a teenager. During the course of the wars, his father passed away.

Edwin was frustrated that he couldn't continue with school once the wars were over, when he and his family returned to Liberia. "Since then, college is not easy here…affordable, I mean." He explained that since his father's death, he had been responsible for taking care of his mother and sister. In order to provide for them, Edwin needed to work on farms and pick produce to earn a living. The house his family owned previously had been burned down and the property eventually taken over by others because it had been abandoned for so long—he and his family had remained in Guinea for over ten years.

Subsequently, I found out that, like Edwin, most of the people who helped us were passing up their usual daily wages to do so. Rather than work on a farm or sell goods in the market, they chose to sacrifice their earnings in order to work at the building site.

"It is our privilege, Sister," Emmanuel said when I shared my concern about them losing some of their income. "You could not keep us away."

"We must be here. You have come so far to do this thing for us," Helena said as she gave her sister a break and tied her nephew on her back using a lappa. Helena was a tall, slender, dark-skinned beauty. She was in her twenties—I asked periodically because so often I was wrong when I tried to guess, and they were unabashed about discussing their age.

"I want to be a doctor, Garmai," Helena said to me during one of our early conversations, her wide smile exposing bright white teeth. She told me that she regularly put away a little of her money from her market earnings and planned to eventually use her savings to go to Monrovia so she could begin college.

Another person talked about saving up to go to high school. The group laughed because he was already in his twenties—even I could see that he was past high school age. However, Mulbah joined in and explained that this was common for two reasons. First, the wars had interrupted the education of the people, and those who were trying to catch up were much older than the typical age for any given grade level. Second, he shared that the government had passed a law that schools—through high school—are free.

However, the people didn't have the ability to enforce that law, particularly in the interior. Apparently, those in charge often instituted various types of "fees" in order to make some money on the side.

"They have to eat too," someone called out.

In addition, others shared that many people couldn't afford the school uniforms or the proper shoes that were required. This was an additional deterrent and often meant the families had to save up in order that their children could attend public school. College, therefore, seemed even further out of sight, nearly impossible, for many. And yet, others remained hopeful at the possibility, cultivating a vision of what could be.

Corruption – The American Way

Saturday, 7/10

What a wonderful day of rest we had! As we did every evening, we sat out on Aunt Kayea's porch and ate our meal. But on this particular night, neither Joseph nor I, with bowl still in hand, nodded off after eating. Early risings coupled with manual labor can do that to you—and it had every other day, all week long. Having taken the day off from work, however, we possessed more energy to sit and talk.

They loved this. Joseph and I were entertainment of sorts. Everything we did seemed to draw attention. When we ate, they were curious as to why we had separate bowls since the people there shared, eating out of one bowl and usually using one spoon. This happened whether or not they were family. At first, I presumed it was because of poverty. *Scarce resources cause such restrictions,* I thought. My assumptions were later confirmed, I believed. "This is what we have," one woman said when I inquired.

The next time we were at the market, Joseph and I bought a few bowls and spoons and gave them to Joseph's family. They smiled and thanked us, and the children showed off their new acquisitions to friends. However, the next morning everyone was back to eating out of one bowl—four of them passed a spoon around the circle. I saw the same behavior at the worksite too. Yes, in part, it might have been because of limited means; it might also have been out of habit; but there was something quite wonderful about the sharing that was so much a part of the Zorzor community.

What he and I ate garnered interest as well. When I noticed that they stared as I ate my dessert, a handful of trail mix, I offered the bag. First, there were smiles, then close investigation with their eyes of what I offered. Next, there was exploration with hands—fingering the cranberries, coconut shavings, and almonds—before passing it to their mouths. Finally, they smiled, and with each chew, their eyes widened.

"Sister, I like it," Rose finally said.

"Garmai, it is good," Aunt Kayea proclaimed, smiling from ear to ear and holding out her hand for more.

"Come, come," I heard nine-year-old Zizi calling to her friends. She didn't want them to miss out on the treat, and they eagerly responded to her beckoning.

Joseph teasingly whispered to me, "They're not going to be able to eat peanuts after this."

Peanuts are plentiful in Zorzor. It is a very common snack, and people walk around with baskets of them—raw or roasted—for sale. During the week, those from the town often came by the building site and gave us handfuls, another "tank you" of sorts.

Joseph's reference had been to a couple occurrences earlier in the week. One morning, I just couldn't eat rice for breakfast. I had graciously accepted it on several mornings, but by the fourth day, I simply wasn't up for it. I do like rice, but not every day for breakfast, lunch, and dinner. I know that sounds very spoiled of me, but it's the truth. So, I pulled out my peanut butter. Yes, I had brought peanut butter all the way from Poughkeepsie, New York to Zorzor, Liberia. Although Joseph said that Monrovia had most of the things we would need, he was clear that it would be different "up country" in Zorzor. Not wanting to take any chances, I packed my peanut butter and lots of trail mix in my suitcase. I also brought along bread from Monrovia, just in case. Though a tad stale, it was still palatable.

That morning, when we settled onto our usual seats of overturned buckets and Aunt Kayea took the pot off the coals to dish my rice, I said, "No thank you. I have something else this morning." All eyes— of the group of six or seven who lived there and waited to eat breakfast with us each day—became fixed on me. I went about spreading peanut butter on slices of bread and served them. Then, I ate a few of my own. They smiled, I smiled, and when I offered up the spoon with a big scoop of peanut butter, the children looked at each other, and the spoon vanished from sight within the circle of beaming faces.

Well, the next morning when we arrived at the backyard kitchen for breakfast, there was the usual welcome party of little ones and grown-ups. Except for Zizi, the kids shared their bowl of rice and tobogi. Zizi looked rather sad and sat off to the side.

"Zizi, not hungry this morning?" I asked. She shook her head but didn't look up.

"Is she okay?" I asked her grandmother.

She smiled at me and snapped something to her granddaughter in Loma. The little girl looked up at her, responded, and then looking back at the ground, shook her head again.

Old Lady was hanging clothes on the line and interjected, "She said she will only eat peanut butter and bread for breakfast…no more rice."

"Oh Lord…" I said, looking at Joseph who was already eating his bowl of rice. "I've corrupted them with my American ways."

"You just had to have peanut butter and bread," Joseph replied between his spoonfuls.

Well, I tried to right the wrong I had done and reached for a bowl of rice, hoping it would be a matter of "out of sight, out of mind" for Zizi, but I couldn't do it. *Why shouldn't she enjoy it while it's available?* I questioned. I reached into my bag, pulled out the peanut butter and the few remaining slices of bread, called Zizi over, and we delighted in our breakfast.

By the end of the week, a similar thing happened at the worksite with Junior, the twelve-year-old. He sat with his head in his hands, looking quite dejected. I asked his father why his previously-animated son looked so unhappy. Throughout the week he had been running back and forth to complete every errand given him, was always eager to help with the building, and brought me cucumbers each day.

"He's thirsty," the father responded.

"Oh, but we have plenty of water." I started to walk toward the cooler to get one of the bags of water. It was still early in the day, and I knew there would be lots left. I couldn't imagine why Junior would be allowed to remain thirsty.

"No, no, Sister…it is not the water he wants," the father called out to me. "He said he wants water from the bottle." The others in earshot let out a laugh.

"From the bottle?" For a moment I was confused.

He pointed to the bottles off to the side, the ones Joseph and I had brought with us from Monrovia and drank throughout the day at the warnings that we should not drink the local water from the well.

"Oh!" I smiled as I thought, *Here we go again.* "Come," I called out to Junior. When he saw me holding up the bottle, he ran over. We both plopped down to the ground, and I offered him the water.

"Tank you, Garmai," Junior held the bottle up to his head and quenched his thirst. I pulled him close and kissed the top of his head. I knew once we were gone, there would be no more bottled water. For the time being, though, it was within my power to satisfy his longing.

Sitting on the porch that Saturday night, I was happy, tickled really, as were our new friends. I watched as the oldest among them, in her late sixties, exploded with the same excitement as the youngest, a five-year-old neighbor, when they encountered something foreign and delicious. I didn't realize just how thrilled some people, children and adults alike, could be about things that are so commonplace to the rest of us.

"What is it called?" Rose asked, squinting from the tartness of the red chewy things she had saved for her last bites.

"Cranberries," I said, offering another handful.

Perhaps, I corrupted a few with my American ways, though I hope not. Looking back, it was worth the possibility knowing I'd provided some moments of delight.

Chapter Seven

As the days passed and I interacted with more of the folks from Zorzor and the neighboring counties, I continued to experience a cultural awakening, and perhaps they did too. They were amused when I marveled at how the women effortlessly wrapped lappas to carry babies on their backs as they continued to carry on with life. They giggled when I stopped along the road to watch the strength of the children, women, and men who carried hefty loads on their heads. They were mystified when I questioned the far distance they walked daily to get life's tasks completed.

The fact is, though I considered myself hardworking and a minimalist in terms of my accumulation of material things, my life was so markedly different from theirs. Though I thought myself fairly well-versed on many social issues, I was surprised that our worlds seemed so far apart. And yet, there were recurring moments when I was brought back to how closely linked our global worlds are too. Like in Monrovia, when Linda and Seplu picked us up in a white SUV dressed in t-shirts and jeans, or while parked in Banga, when I saw a group of boys on their motorbikes dressed in leather jackets and leather gloves trying to outmaneuver each other. Or even as I walked down the main road in Zorzor and saw someone wearing a "Got Milk?" t-shirt or a different item of clothing with another western slogan or logo. The differences and similarities were all very confusing and sometimes laughable. Occasionally, their parroting of western ways made me sad, too, because those behaviors were not necessarily good and certainly not better than their own native ones.

The consistent difference was that they didn't judge. They didn't assume that "our western way," is bad, inferior, or wrong. In fact, some accepted that it's better—almost idealizing the foreign—particularly all things American. More often, most were simply curious. They eagerly asked questions and excitedly waited for the responses that would give them some understanding of the new thing or a different approach. It's certainly a quality I want to adopt and hope to pass on to others.

This Part of the Sky – False Notions

Monday, 7/12

The one day I was sick, I apparently missed some rousing conversation at the work site. While everyone continued to work, I feasted on bottled water, Echinacea, raw garlic, and cayenne pepper all day—the natural remedies I had packed in my suitcase along with what Old Lady added. The combination knocked the ailment right out of my system, so by evening, I was feeling much better. I wasn't ready to start eating solid foods, but I had enough energy to want to be in the company of our friends.

We had already previously delayed our leave by a couple of days to allow Joseph the time he needed to follow up on supplies that hadn't yet arrived and make the last payments for some of the other materials. This had been arranged in an attempt to complete as much of the building as possible before we had to leave. We knew we were so close to the end and wanted to see the finished product. However, knowing we needed to return to the states, we had set our departure for two days later to get us to Monrovia in advance of our flight from Liberia. I didn't want to miss out on any of our remaining time together in Zorzor.

Joseph and I took our usual walk over to Aunt Kayea's in the evening. As we walked, he told me about the discussions earlier in the day. "Baby, they idealize America so much...everything about it," he said, shaking his head.

"Yeah," I responded, thinking back to a conversation I'd had with his cousin. Large signs, billboard-like, were posted to stop the abuse of girls and women—an issue that had escalated during and since the wars. Old Lady mentioned that the signs had been put up by the government at the request of President Sirleaf. She was astounded to hear me say that this was a problem in America too. "No," she said, shaking her head. "Women cannot be hurt in America." I simply couldn't convince her.

Joseph continued. "We talked about everything from homeless people...they laughed when I said there are people in the U.S. living on the streets."

"That must have been a shock," I responded.

"Yeah. Then we started talking about how some people drop out of high school and don't go to college, and they couldn't believe it..."

"Because so many of them are desperate for the opportunity to go to school," I finished Joseph's sentence.

"Then, swatting flies, Emmanuel said to me, 'Oh, it must be nice to be in America where there are no flies.'" Joseph shook his head again. "I couldn't stop laughing…can you believe that? Some of the other guys laughed too, but I didn't know if they were joking or serious. You know, some of the older guys—Mulbah, Dennis, Bedell—who've gone to Monrovia or across the borders to Guinea or Ghana, know better. They're more realistic than the ones who have never left the interior."

I started to think about how similar that is elsewhere too—including in America—a consistent building up of one culture as superior and ideal, which leaves other people and places inferior. Sometimes it left me feeling sad, at other times overwhelmed. How do we burst those bubbles that hold such false notions? How do we stop the portrayal of partial images in America and the rest of the western world about Africa, Asia, and other developing countries? And, how do we extinguish the idea that our worlds, those of industrialized countries, are much better off and ideal even—in culture or in value?

I realized that the disappointment I had felt when

I first arrived in Monrovia was because another culture had been adopted; I preferred to see the native dress and local ways of doing things. This was akin to having been in Buenos Aires a few years earlier and seeing McDonald's restaurants every few blocks along the way; it didn't matter that the menu was in Spanish or the portion sizes were significantly less. Though I did give in once to my Achilles' heel—fries—the fact is, I don't want to visit another country and get what I can get on any given day in America.

Yet, even though I was keenly aware of the incomplete picture rendered abroad, I'd still had some misperceptions when I arrived in Liberia. It was good to be there and get a more complete picture about the range of experiences in the Liberian people's lives. Yes, indeed, there were some in the interior who did not wear shoes, but there were others in Monrovia who donned suits and ties. While some sat in circles on the ground to eat out of one bowl, others sat in chairs at a table set with plates, forks, and knives.

I couldn't offer a trip to the United States to our friends in Zorzor, so I hoped for opportunities to give them a more realistic picture of life here. Yes, there are people who pick out of garbage bins for food in America. And women are abused in America. At the least, whenever possible, I looked for occasions to express my admiration for the people of Zorzor and their culture.

As was usual, we had several people dine on the porch with us that evening. Others stopped by to say they had missed me at the worksite and were praying for me to feel better. They hoped it wasn't malaria or yellow fever. I assured them I was well.

As they walked us back to our sleeping quarters, I pulled out my flashlight—just as I had done on previous nights. Usually, unless we walked by someone's porch or shop where a generator powered a light bulb in the area, it was difficult to see where we were going. I paused before turning it on, realizing I didn't really need the light. At first, I thought it had to be that my eyes were getting more accustomed to the dark. Or perhaps I was just less exhausted, since I had been in bed most of the day. Joseph must have caught my pondering, because in that moment he told me to look up. Gazing up at the sky, I was brought to a complete standstill.

"Wow!" I exclaimed. "Look how bright and beautiful it is up there!"

"Sister, they are stars," someone whispered in the semi-dark. Some chuckling followed.

"They light up the sky," I added as I continued to gaze upward."

"Garmai, there are no stars in America?"

I had to resist the urge to laugh out loud. I thought to say, *"Yes, we have stars in America, but they are all covered by smog."* Or, *"Yes, but we make ourselves so busy that we don't have time to look up at them."* Instead, anticipating what their next questions might be, I kept it simple: "Yes, there are stars in America. But none that shine so bright as here, in this part of the sky."

My response was enough to satisfy; no other questions followed. In fact, I sensed a slight pep in their steps and glimpsed grins across a few faces. I was glad for it.

Chapter Eight

Farewell, My Friends

Wednesday, 7/14

"Sister, you will make us cry," Anthony, the head builder, said to me as he looked away.

It was the afternoon before our departure and we were taking lots of pictures at the site. We laughed as we posed and sang songs. Joseph and I gave away our clothes, boots, work gloves, and other items we had bought specifically for the trip. Later that evening, I gave the last of my trail mix and peanut butter to Aunt Kayea and the children. Though we wanted to see the entire building completed, the cement needed to cure before they could put on the rafters or roof.

We were pleased and amazed that they had put the building up in eight days.

As much as we wanted to stay until the work was truly completed, we knew we couldn't delay our trip any longer—we were already limiting ourselves to just a few more days in Monrovia with Joseph's brother and other extended family before leaving Liberia for home. Though we had considered it, we couldn't afford to reschedule our flight out of the country. We had spent every penny of the funds we'd raised and more of our own. And so it was, in the words of my husband, "Time to go home."

The morning we left Zorzor to head back to Monrovia, I was the one moved to tears as one after the other gathered on the porch where I had first met most of them. I smiled and blinked over and over to keep my tears at bay. Edwin handed me something wrapped in paper. "It is special for you—country cloth from Guinea…to make a blouse for you or your mother."

Another cousin of Joseph's—one of the wives of the Muslim neighbor further down the road—presented her hat. I had complimented the fine threading a few days earlier. She refused to take no for an answer. "She'll be insulted if you don't take it," Joseph warned.

"Garmai...for your trip," Bedell handed me a package. His wife had made another cake for me to take on our trip; I had jokingly licked my fingers after eating one before.

We formed a circle, held hands, and Dennis prayed.

"Brother, come back to us," one person said softly.

"Sister, do not forget us," another whispered. *That's not possible*, I thought, on the verge of sobbing.

"No, we won't," I managed to say as Joseph and I walked hand-in-hand to the car, not yet ready to begin the ride back to Monrovia. It didn't faze me that we were packed liked sardines, having agreed to let a few people travel to Monrovia with us. This time, I was not troubled by the unpaved road. I didn't fret about needing to go to the bathroom. Instead, my mind was occupied with the goodbyes and "tank yous."

Our trip passed in silence. Gone was the anticipation, ripe during our travel to Zorzor. We were not yet able to replace the trip back with a sense of contentment or satisfaction. "Maybe it's because we didn't see the roof on?" I pondered out loud to Joseph, trying to understand the malaise I was feeling, which I saw mirrored in his face. He didn't say much in response.

In actuality, I was already missing them. The work we had planned for so long was done. Sure, we would find ways to be in touch from time to time. We would continue to send some assistance to improve the building and get the school running. Joseph had already been inquiring about the salary for a teacher and given the elders tips on how to go door-to-door to get the children enrolled. We even planned to return to add to the school portion and build a playground on the premises.

However, as we continued toward Monrovia and the distance widened between us and Zorzor, I began to understand that we were moving further away from not only the people I'd come to love but so much more. We were leaving the everyday conversations, all-day contact, meals and laughter shared together, and time spent learning to know and understand each other more deeply. It felt as if we were heading toward absolutely nothing—a sinking emptiness. The accomplishment of completing the building project was overshadowed by the gloom of saying farewell to our friends—our brothers and sisters. Yes, I was missing them. So great had been their impact.

From time to time, someone now finds me daydreaming—reminiscing about the stories, meals, and time shared with those in Zorzor. They hear me laugh out loud as I recall how serious and determined I was about figuring out a way to climb into that barrel of water when I first arrived. They see me grimace as I remember the pain of carrying the concrete block on my head. They see me smile as I see in my mind's eye the delight of eating peanut butter with all those children. Putting up a building was actually a small part of my time in Liberia. Constructing relationships was an even greater portion of it.

Epilogue

Over the last two years, we've communicated with the folks in Zorzor via phone calls and email and letters exchanged through people visiting Liberia. As expected, the enthusiasm and hard work of the people of Zorzor did not wane after we left. On the Sabbath following our departure, they abandoned their mud hut church and worshipped in the new structure, even though it was still unfinished. Within weeks, they had added finishing touches to the building, as they continue to do. At last report, there are over ninety people regularly meeting at the church and the building is also used as a community space.

Our first call came from Dennis who said it was still unbelievable to the people there that we had come and done such "a work" for them. He shared that people from all over the county were coming to look at the building. Apparently, even some folks from Monrovia had made the trip to see the new church. In fact, we also received a call from a pastor based in Monrovia who was visiting relatives in D.C. He wanted to say "tank you" for our efforts, as he had had an opportunity to visit with the people in Zorzor and see the building for himself.

We were also told that the children of those who were involved in the work had started to attend the school. Then, some of the elders went door-to-door to invite others from the town to send their children. They made sure that parents were aware they wouldn't have to be concerned about paying fees or having their children wear uniforms or proper shoes, as was often the case at the government schools. Their yield was great—about thirty children began to attend.

However, the rainy season continued through several months and hit them hard. Sometime in November of that first year, Emmanuel called to say that the area was flooded; the new building was not damaged but the makeshift road had been destroyed. As a result, they had to temporarily suspend the school, though the adults were determined to get there for worship services and community meetings no matter what.

Over the last year, there have been so many gains. Mulbah emailed to tell us that he felt called to make the sacrifice to go back to school. He is now enrolled at Liberia University in Monrovia. Emmanuel, Helena, and another from the core group also passed the West African Examination—a major exam that qualifies individuals to go to college. Scholarships are based on their results. All three are planning to attend the university.

Indeed, they continue to look for ways to better themselves, to improve their circumstances, and to offer opportunities to their children—no less than others do. They also continue to look for means and ways to add to the building, pave the road, add to the school section, and see the goal realized of all that we dreamt together. We continue to send whatever funds we can. Though we had planned to return two years later—in the summer of 2012—to build a separate school and playground, we found it unrealistic with a new addition to our family. Joseph and I decided we did want to have children, and thankfully, we were blessed. The next time we return, we will bring with us Leah Garmai—our daughter—to continue building.

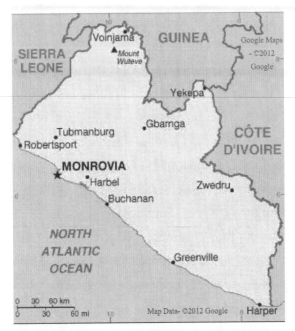

Map of Liberia

Joseph and me in Liberia

The beach was walking distance from
my in-laws' house in Monrovia

Monrovia is a thriving city. Featured is
the Temple of Justice - the courthouse

My in-laws' home in Monrovia

I'm under that mosquito net and
have another beside me to cover up with

The outhouse I barely escaped from
because a lizard was in hot pursuit of me

The bumpy road we traveled for eight hours from
Monrovia to Zorzor, which left us with three flat tires

People came to welcome us at the
mud hut church in Zorzor

Aunt Kayea

Rose

Zizi and a neighbor friend

Emmanuel

Aunt Kayea put down a welcome mat
for me at the entrance of her home

The Business Women's Association
of Zorzor sang and danced

Joseph and Anthony, the chief builder,
made plans for the foundation

Everyone joined in doing the work,
including 12-year-old Junior

The strong women of Zorzor were
actively involved in the work

Kloboh kept an eye on me as I struggled
to carry blocks to the building site

In groups
at the
building
site we
took a break
for meals

We took a half-day break to visit The Teacher Training
Institute in Fissebu where Joseph's parents met

Fissebu - a palm tree paradise

Jelly coconuts - an edible delight

As in other countries, many listened to the radio and
awaited the results of the FIFA World Cup 2010

We gathered at the mud hut for a farewell

We said goodbye to the core group working at the site

The new building - now being used as a
church, school and community space

The Power of You

Many people have said, "What a great thing you and Joseph did for those people." They've exclaimed, "How charitable of you!" Really, it was neither. It was truly a matter of honoring a connection that we have, which you have too. We share a human bond—brothers and sisters on this earth. In addition, it was not as challenging to plan this work as some may think and it didn't require six-figure-income jobs.

The fact is, Joseph and I aspire to live a life that is in part based on the question, "What do you want your legacy to be?" It is not meant to be answered, as one friend put it, "from a place of vanity, but from a place of humanity."

So, what do you want your legacy to be? You can do this too and make a difference in the lives of others. I promise, your life will also be changed in the process.

It really isn't that difficult to get started. I've put together a list, along with some of what Joseph and I learned along the way, to help you begin.

1. Decide on a community you want to assist and with which you feel a connection—locally or abroad. I'm convinced that we do our best when we are personally invested. So, choose work you are genuinely passionate about, work that will keep you connected to your values. To discover what is meaningful for you, you might need to journal—finding a quiet place and space in your life to think on the matter—or make a list of the recent news stories that have moved you.

Our story: Joseph and I were connected to the work in Liberia because it is his birthplace. For us, there was and still is a strong family connection as well as our belief in the importance of people having a space to worship as they choose and our commitment to the importance of a free education.

2. Develop a vision for what exactly it is that you want to do. Be clear and precise about the work you are endeavoring to accomplish. Write a basic plan, which should include the end result you want to see.

Our story: Joseph first wrote down how much money would be needed after he got estimates of what it would cost to put up a building in Zorzor and the steps necessary to complete the work—both the planning in New York and the constructing in Zorzor. He also set a $10,000 goal, which I must admit I initially told him was an unrealistic amount for the two of us to raise. However, it was based on the estimated costs he had researched.

3. Share your goals and vision with the right people. You know who the people are in your life that will cheer for you, offer to help, and/or connect you with others who can move your vision forward. Choose those people to speak with about your plans. Perhaps, have one or two others to whom you can be accountable—those willing for you to check in with about how things are proceeding.

Our story: We had decided to start a special savings account where we would continue to put a little money aside to send to Zorzor. We knew the money would first be used to buy the land and then we would continue to offer what we could to help with getting the building constructed. As we shared with family and friends, they offered to donate. Many informed others and even gave us ideas for fundraising events. A week before we left for Liberia, we had reached the $10, 000 goal. We did it together, with the help of a supportive community.

4. Respect the *Law of Gestation**. There is a certain amount of time needed for a seed to grow into a tree.* Don't rush brilliance. Take action, manage each task one step at a time, but let the work take the time it needs to be life transforming—for others and for you.

Our story: This project didn't come together overnight. It began with a simple plan to give a community some assistance. The initial thought to send a donation grew into a larger endeavor. It took time to write a proposal that we could hand to interested people. Focusing on each fundraising event often felt like a project in and of itself. Each opportunity to talk about the project—gearing up for a presentation to a rotary club, a church congregation, or at a community event—took energy and effort. Even the last phase of the project, doing the actual work in Zorzor, couldn't be rushed. Because of the rain and the time the structure needed to cure, we would have done harm to put the roof up too soon or add other finishing touches just so we could see the finished product before we left Liberia.

5. Get your hands dirty. This should be an opportunity to use your skills. Make good use of what you are good at doing. However, don't mistake activity for productivity.

Our story: The work has been fulfilling, by far, because we literally got involved. An avid rider, Joseph started out by doing a 100-mile bike ride to raise funds that purchased the land. I did most of the speaking at events. I also tracked the funds as they came in and sent thank you notes each time we got a donation. Joseph also used his architectural and civil engineering skills to draw plans for the building and assess the materials needed. And he used his baking skills to supply goodies for the bake sales. Finally, we both agreed that we needed to make the trip— to be accountable for the funds, and especially, to participate in the work.

Your turn: Okay, what are you waiting for? Make your mark on the world! Go forth and do great things!

"Not everybody can be famous
but everybody can be great because
greatness is determined by service."
— Martin Luther King, Jr.

About the Author

Wendy Maragh Taylor is a writer, speaker and licensed clinical social worker. She has worked with individuals, families and groups through community-based organizations, public schools and colleges/universities for over 15 years. Wendy seeks always to educate and empower people to reach their full potential; this often means helping them find their voice so they can better their lives. She uses her writing to engage, provoke thought and promote healing. She earned her Bachelors from Brown University and her Masters from New York University. Wendy lives in New York with her husband, Joseph, and her baby daughter, Leah Garmai. To learn more about Wendy's other projects or to contact her, visit www.wendymaraghtaylor.com.

A percentage of the proceeds
from the sale of this book will go
to the Liberia Project.